C000101389

John Bosco

by
Jennifer Moorcroft

*All booklets are published thanks to the
generous support of the members of the
Catholic Truth Society*

CATHOLIC TRUTH SOCIETY
PUBLISHERS TO THE HOLY SEE

Contents

Early Life

One day John Bosco told a story. There was a peddler, he said, who was tired out trying to sell his wares, so he settled under a tree to rest. He took out a night cap from his bag, put it on and fell asleep. During the night some monkeys in the trees (for it was monkey country) came down and stole all his stock of night caps and put them on.

The peddler was very annoyed when he woke the following morning to find the monkeys wearing his night caps and gave chase, trying to catch them and get his caps back, but the monkeys were too quick for him. Finally, in frustration, he snatched the cap off his own head and threw it on the ground – and all the monkeys did likewise.

The moral, he said, was that we tend to imitate others, for good or for bad. John was very young when he discovered he had just such a gift of influencing others.

His family

John Bosco was born 16th August 1815 to Francis and Margaret Bosco, and baptised the following day. This was Francis' second marriage, as his first wife had died, leaving a young boy, Anthony, to be brought up with the couple's own two children; Joseph was two years older than John. Francis Bosco's elderly ailing mother, Margaret Zucca, also came to live with them.

The family lived in Becchi, a small hamlet in the Piedmont region of Italy. Francis was a day-labourer with a smallholding that augmented his uncertain wages. Sadly, when John was two years old his father died suddenly of pneumonia. As he lay dying, he asked his wife to take care of the three boys, 'I know you will do your best with the children,' he said, then added, 'Take care of our John in a special way.'

His mother was now forced to be the breadwinner for the whole family who found themselves in even greater poverty. It was the worst possible time, because an exceptionally hot summer had burnt up the crops and people were often at starvation levels. She faced the challenge with a courage that was native to her, and all the family had to play their part. Anthony, at twelve years old, accepted that his role in life would be farming. Even little John was expected to do his bit, at first helping with small tasks around the house, and then from the age of five with looking after their two cows, meeting up with other boys in the pastures above the hamlet.

John's dream

John proved popular with the other boys – or most of them. He had a strong, sturdy body, well able to take care of himself in the fights and rough-and-tumble that inevitably occurred. He came home one day with a gash to his head. He would never explain to his mother what had happened, saying only that it was an accident. His mother forbade him to mix with the bullies, but John pleaded with her, saying that when he was with them 'they do as I want them to do, and don't fight any more.' When he was with them, he added, 'they are better and don't use bad words.'

Already, he was recognising the influence he had over other boys; loving God so much, he hated the boys blaspheming, and of course, some would do so deliberately simply in order to rile him. He would respond with his fists, which would explain the gash on his head.

About this time, he had a dream that explained to him that this was not the way to change his companions' behaviour, and also gave him some understanding of what would be his life's work. Many years later he wrote down this experience at the Pope's request:

At the age of about nine years old I had a dream that remained deeply impressed on my mind for the rest of my life. In the dream I seemed to be near a house in a large courtyard where a crowd of boys were playing together. Some were laughing, others were playing, and many of them were blaspheming.

On hearing these blasphemies I immediately rushed into their midst, raising my voice and using my fists to make them keep quiet. At that moment a dignified-looking man who seemed to be in the prime of life and was nobly clad, appeared on the scene. A white mantle covered the whole of His person, but His face was so radiant that I was unable to look at it for long. He called me by my name and directed me to place myself at the head of these boys, ending with the words, 'You must win the hearts of these friends of yours, not with blows but with sweetness and charity. Set to work at once, then, to instruct them on the wickedness of sin and on the excellence of virtue.'

The man in the dream went on to give him the help of His Mother, who also appeared, majestic in bearing and clad in a mantle of bright light. John explained that he did not understand the meaning of the dream but was assured by the lady, 'In good time, my son, you will understand everything.'

His mother's example

His mother had not only to earn a living to support her family, but also to bring them up in the love of God. They had the best possible example in her, because everything spoke to her of God; He was in the very air she breathed.

Walking in the beautiful countryside she exulted in the wonder of God's creation, exclaiming that if there was so much beauty on earth, what would heaven be like! The whole family gathered three times a day to pray together. She was unable to read, but her mind was richly stocked with stories from the Bible and stories of the saints, and she instinctively drew lessons from the world around her. Faith for her was a joyful thing, so when she reminded her boys, 'God sees us', this was not a threat but a reminder that someone who was all Love was watching over them, and that if they were naughty they were hurting one who loved them without limits.

There was a rod in the corner of the room, but if the boys were honest and owned up then it was not used. One day, in his exuberance John knocked over a bowl of grain; he went out and peeled a switch, handing it to his mother to punish him when she returned home. There was no need. He had confessed and that was enough.

Learning a few tricks

When Margaret went to the local market to sell her meagre produce John often went with her. He was intrigued by the magicians, the acrobats, the funfair buskers who entertained the people among the produce stalls, and studied them closely to learn the tricks of their trade. It is a measure of his intelligence that he was able to work out a conjuring trick for himself; it was a proof of his physical ability that after much practice and perseverance he was able to walk a tightrope, and perform acrobatic tricks. His gift for storytelling and singing he inherited from his mother.

In all this he had an ulterior motive: to win the interest of children and adults alike. He made a bargain with them that if they would say the rosary with him or listen to him for a while as he spoke to them of God, then he would do a conjuring trick for them or a tightrope walk. The adults would grumble a little, but then give in with good grace at the prospect of the entertainment to follow. Gradually, though, children and adults alike would find that he made everything enjoyable, for what could be more joy-giving than experiencing the life and winsomeness of God?

He was sensitive towards others. There was one boy, from a family as poor as his, who brought coarse black bread to eat. Margaret made good bread for her family so John looked at the other boy's bread and said he liked the look of it, could they swap? They did so and after that John ate the hard bread.

No favourites

Margaret loved her three sons equally, although sometimes it must have been hard. Anthony took over when his stepmother was away at the market, but the other two boys refused to obey him. Joseph, who was a little slow, would eventually give way, but John would not, ending in fisticuffs. Their mother returned home one day to find a fight in full swing, with Anthony badly hurting the two younger ones. She scolded him, and he taunted her, 'Step-mother, Step-mother!'

'I have always treated you as my own son, you can't deny that,' she confronted him squarely. 'I have the right and the strength to correct you, but I won't. Now, hit your mother!' Of course, he did not, but he still bitterly resented John, whom his grandmother described as being like quicksilver.

Margaret would have been forgiven for preferring her youngest son, but she did not. One day John and Joseph came into the house for a drink of water. She gave a drink to Joseph first and John sulked, refusing it when she offered it to him in turn. He came to her a little while afterwards, again asking for a drink.

'I thought you weren't thirsty!'

'I am now. I'm sorry for the way I acted.'

'And you know I love you and Joseph equally. Tell Our Lord you're sorry, and here's your drink.'

Can I be a priest?

Telling his family later about the dream he had had, John asked them what they thought it meant. 'You'll be a peasant farmer?' suggested Joseph. 'The chief of brigands,' sneered Anthony. 'A priest?' asked his mother quietly. Already she was noticing how advanced John was in his understanding of the Faith. At that time children did not receive Holy Communion until the age of twelve, but the parish priest agreed that he should make his First Communion when he was ten years old. His mother prepared him for that great day. The nearest church was at Castelnuovo, six miles away. This is one reason why his talks about the faith to the children filled an urgent gap: many did not want to make the long journey. He made his First Communion shortly after Easter Day, having prepared for it in prayer and reflection.

The following month, in April, there was a mission in Buttigleria, ten miles away, and John walked there and back, thinking and praying about what he had heard at the mission. One evening on the way home Don Calosso, an elderly priest from Murialdo, noticed the thoughtful boy and started talking to him. He was amazed to find that John could not only reproduce the morning's sermon but it was evident that he understood it. Discovering John's desire to become a priest Don Calosso took him under his wing and supplemented his meagre schooling with further lessons, especially in Latin, that would better prepare him for the priesthood.

The arrangement was that John would study with the gentle, kindly priest in the morning and help out on the farm in the afternoon, but this arrangement did not meet with Anthony's approval, who now saw himself as head of the household. It enraged him to see his step-brother studying his books at every opportunity, although John never shirked his tasks around the farm. Anthony and Joseph were destined to be peasant farmers, why should John be any different? The atmosphere became so bad, Anthony became so violent towards John, that John gave up his studies until the autumn so that he could help with the harvest. Even this did not pacify his step-brother, and their mother realised that the only way to bring some semblance of peace and harmony to the family was for John to leave home.

A new life

In February 1829, when he was fourteen, John left home to seek work, his precious books in his knapsack. It was the worst possible time, the middle of winter, to look for farm work, but his mother had suggested the Moglia farm, near Moncucco, as she knew the family. They were charitable and successful; perhaps they could take in a poor unskilled labourer without too much harm to their finances. It took a lot of persuading, but eventually Dorothy, the farmer's wife, began to feel sorry for the lad and persuaded her husband to take him on for a few days' trial.

John proved such a valuable asset that he was soon given a salary and stayed for two years. He was later to describe this period as 'the loveliest and most romantic time' of his life. Besides working on the farm, he looked after the Moglia's three-year old son, Luigi, who, unsurprisingly, followed John everywhere. He also won the approval of Don Cottino, the parish priest, who gave him permission to instruct the young children of the parish. He was being given a growing awareness that this was to be his life's work. And he continued his studies in the tiny attic cupboard that was his room, stifling in summer, freezing in winter.

Deep down, though, John knew he could not stay indefinitely with the Moglias if he was to pursue his dream. Help came to him in the form of an uncle, Margaret's brother, Michael Occhiena, who had made some money in cattle-raising. He visited the Moglia farm and met with John, who poured out his difficulties to him. Michael came to an instant decision, and told John to pack his bags, much to the Moglia family's sadness, since they had grown very fond of him.

The two of them returned to Becchi to discuss John's future. With Anthony just as violently opposed to John continuing his studies as before, their mother intervened and forcefully declared her decision. The small family heritage would be divided up between the three boys. Anthony went to another family farm nearby; Joseph and his mother would stay in the Becchi farm; John went to board with his old mentor Don Calosso and continued his studies.

There was a deep bond of love and affection between the two, and the ailing Don Calosso intended to provide for his young protégé after his death, which was not long in coming. He left six thousand lire for John that would help in his seminary studies, but relatives descended on the house as soon as he was dead and took the lot. John did not protest, but returned to the family farm, grieving deeply for his beloved master and worried about the future.

Towards the Priesthood

In his grief and despair, John had another dream in which he was rebuked for putting his trust in man and not in God. John trusted, but it was hard. He continued to study Latin in Castelnuova, walking the twelve miles there and back each day, his shoes slung over his shoulder to save the leather, until his mother arranged for him to lodge in town with a tailor, Robert Gioanni. He was older and bigger than the rest of the students and was mocked by the students as being stupid, a country bumpkin, a judgment shared by his teacher who called him an ass and asked whether anything good could come out of Becchi. It was a lesson in humility for him.

At the tailor's house he earned his keep by learning how to sew, making waistcoats, breeches and underwear.

The student

His mother realised that he was not doing well at his studies, and with her accustomed determination arranged for him to start the following term at a college in Chieri.

It was a successful change for him. His lodgings were wretched but his studies took off. He had an outstandingly retentive memory which increasingly stood him in good stead. One day he forgot his Latin textbook, and when called on to do the translation he not only reproduced his translation from memory, but also the Latin text, something that his stunned classmates quietly pointed out to the master afterwards. Another time, he had a dream which gave him the translation of a text that they studied the following day.

In Chieri, he had several lodgings and in each of them, to earn his keep, he learnt new skills; a friend of the family, Piana, owned a café, and there John learnt how to make all kinds of sweets, cordials, and ice creams. Elsewhere, he worked as a blacksmith, a carpenter and tutoring the children of the various households. Although he did not realise it at the time, he was adding to his experience and everything would prove to be of value later on.

Society of Joy

Starting in the bottom grade, John soon made his way up into the top grades, where he should have been, and he also made his way into the hearts of his fellow students. He began a group that met to pray together, discuss the gospel of the day, attend church services, and pray the rosary. He called his group the "Society of Joy", and it truly was a group characterised by their cheerfulness and enjoyment of life. They would go out together, bundles on their backs to explore the countryside and enjoy each other's company.

Early on he had discerned which boys would be receptive, and he excluded those who would only be a disruptive element by their swearing, obscenities and general criminality. He was not always a model of patience with them when they caused chaos in class before the master arrived. They jumped on the desks hurling their books around, throwing pieces of chalk and pellets at each other, with John powerless to keep order, even though he caught one of the boys and swung him round like a battering ram. He noticed just one boy who sat quietly at his desk while a classmate urged him to join in the mayhem, threatening to hit him if he didn't. 'Hit me if you like,' the boy replied, and his tormentor duly obliged. 'Are you satisfied now?' he asked quietly. 'I forgive you. Now leave me alone.'

The boy was Luigi Comollo. We look to the saints for our inspiration, forgetting that perhaps they also drew inspiration from others on their journey to holiness. So it was with John, who saw in Luigi the greatest example for him to follow: in forbearance, strength, gentleness and prayer, that he perceived as being in such contrast to his own natural character. The two became the greatest of friends and for John it was the deepest friendship of his life.

Seminarian

The holiness he perceived in Luigi brought to a head John's aspiration towards the priesthood. But should he pursue his vocation in the cloister or the secular priesthood? If he wanted to live the life of prayer he saw in Luigi, then he felt he could live that for himself only in the cloister, as a Franciscan. Also, as a member of a religious order he need not worry about the expense of going through the seminary. However, the parish priest of Castelnuovo, with whom he discussed his plans, introduced him to a saintly, newly ordained priest, Don Cafasso, who stated categorically that John should study for the secular priesthood. John remembered that he had met him briefly some years before at a *festa* in Murialdo, and had been much impressed by him.

Reassured, John set to and begged for the necessary funds; friends provided him with the clothing he needed, and in the autumn of 1835 he put on the soutane of a seminarian. He wrote down the resolutions he intended to keep as a seminarian:

he would give up acrobatics, hunting, the violin and other pursuits he considered unbecoming to the priestly state;

he would be abstemious in eating and drinking;

read only books on spirituality and theology;

give himself much to prayer, meditation and spiritual reading;

preserve his chastity in thought, word and deed.

He had the continuing guidance and friendship of Don (now Blessed) Cafasso, and to his great joy, Luigi Comollo also entered the seminary a few months later. During the summer breaks Luigi would join him in the fields, and the parish priest of Capriglio sometimes asked them to preach. Luigi was reticent, but John was only too pleased to be asked. To begin with he used the rather forced rhetorical style of the period and no-one understood him. 'When you speak to the simple,' the priest advised him, 'speak simply.' He might now be well educated and steeped in the classics and theology, but with this advice he would always wear his learning lightly and speak in straightforward ways that spoke to the heart.

To his great sorrow his friendship with Luigi ended only four years into their training. On the Feast of the Annunciation 1839 Luigi's frail body was seized with a pernicious fever and he died peacefully on the Tuesday after Easter.

Ordination

Passing his studies *Summa cum Laude* John was ordained priest on 5th June 1841, the eve of the Feast of the Most Holy Trinity, in the private chapel of the Archbishop of Turin. He said his first Mass the following day in the church of Saint Francis of Assisi, at which only Don Cafasso was present. He was profoundly impressed when he attended Masses celebrated by a contemporary, Blessed Antonio Rosmini. 'I do not recall seeing any priest say Mass with such devotion as Don Rosmini,' he recalled. 'One could experience his most lively faith, source of his charity, goodness, modesty and exterior gravity. I have seen how the saints celebrate the divine sacrifice.' No less could be said of his own celebration of Mass. Blessed Rosmini also became a good benefactor to him.

Then he returned home to be with his family. His mother greeted him with tears of joy, but with realism. 'Remember what I tell you, my son. To begin to say Mass is to begin to suffer. You will see it soon.'

He now had to decide where he should exercise his priestly ministry. Don Cafasso suggested that he should begin at the Convitto, an Ecclesiastical College near the church of Saint Francis of Assisi that provided support and guidance to young priests lost in the vastness of Turin, but which also trained them to be 'shock troops' as it were. They went into prisons, visited the poor, taught catechism, supported the regular parish priests in their ministry, all supported by a life of prayer and study. This missionary outreach was badly needed because Turin was expanding rapidly, with men and boys pouring into the city to find work in the construction industry. Great wealth was fuelling the city's growth, but underneath was the inevitable poverty, crime and deprivation.

The first Salesian

John made his way through this underclass where priests were more often than not greeted with blasphemies and insults. He was inevitably drawn towards the boys who mostly lived by thieving and corruption, trying not to show his repugnance to the filth and squalor. He came from the poorest of backgrounds, but his mother had always made sure that their home was spotlessly clean. He was horrified that boys as young as eight years old worked on these construction sites, toiling as bricklayers, plasterers, carpenters, exposed to all the extremes of weather, carrying heavy loads up rickety scaffolding.

His attempts to speak to them gently and courteously met with blank stares and blasphemy, but he persisted day after day without success. Then, one day on the Feast of the Immaculate Conception, Our Lady gave him the breakthrough he prayed for. He was vesting for Mass at the Convitto when a ragged and dirty boy came to the sacristy. The sacristan asked him whether he had come to serve Mass and when the boy told him he didn't know how to, he berated him as a vagabond and a thief, banged him on the head with a broom and shut the door on him. John quickly came round to see what the commotion was and made the sacristan bring the now tearful vagabond back to him. He invited the boy to stay for Mass and questioned him gently afterwards. The boy was fifteen years old, from Asti, an orphan working as a bricklayer. He could neither read nor write and could not go to catechism classes as he would be laughed at by the younger boys.

'Would you like me to teach you?' asked John, and when the boy said he was eager to learn they sat down together for their first lesson. The boy was Bartholomew Garelli, the first Salesian. He was also the first Salesian missionary, because on the following Sunday he turned up again with six more ragged boys. By the beginning of February there were twenty, by the Feast of the Annunciation, thirty. They met in a room behind the sacristy which had once been a yard; a vine still grew in the middle of the room, hung with grapes.

Their religious instruction was enlivened by games, with John joining in, and proved so popular that soon there were more than a hundred boys. The room was now too small for them and they moved into a courtyard of the Convitto, where they stayed for three years.

The work grows

John's three year period at the Convitto came to an end and he began to think about where he should go next – perhaps to the mission field. Again, it was Don Cafasso who dissuaded him, insisting that his mission was at home, especially in Turin. He was appointed chaplain to an orphanage, the Refuge, run by the Marchesa di Barolo, that enabled him to carry on his work with the boys in his spare time.

The Marchesa was French born, devoting her wealth to charitable works with steely determination that all should be done according to her wishes and not otherwise. She agreed that he should transfer his Oratory, as his group of boys were now called, to part of the Refuge complex. There were now a hundred and fifty boys and even their extended quarters were no longer large enough since they soon doubled in number. John never dampened their exuberance and the Marchesa was soon driven to distraction by the noise they made, especially as the gardener, trying to establish a garden nearby, complained when his prize plants were picked or trampled on searching for a stray ball. They had to move again.

This time it was a piece of ground surrounding a chapel near a cemetery. Now it was the priest's housekeeper who complained about the noise and disruption. Nobody wanted them, wherever they tried to establish themselves. John would take his band out to the countryside or to a field, with boys playing a trumpet, a drum and a guitar leading the way, where they could picnic and enjoy themselves. However, as winter drew near they desperately needed somewhere permanent, where neighbours would not complain. It was not only the noise, but also that some of the boys would revert to their old ways of thieving and bad behaviour. They found various temporary shelters over the winter but by now the city was turning against him. Don Borel, another of his priest advisors, said that he should keep only a few of his boys, the best behaved, and the Governor of Turin demanded that he should dissolve his band, now numbering four hundred. The Marchesa gave him an ultimatum – her orphanage or his Oratory. For Don Bosco there was no contest. He had in mind his vision of years before, of a great band of boys, his lambs, of swarms of children, and had no intention of limiting his horizons.

Tricking the asylum

It was therefore decided that this dreamer, this visionary, was indeed mad, and should be sent away 'for a rest' in an asylum. Two respectable priests were sent to him in a carriage, and after exchanging pleasantries, the priests suggested that they should go for a drive in the carriage. Don Bosco agreed that a little air would do him good and courteously insisted that the two priests precede him into the carriage. He then slammed the door on them, shouted to the driver 'Full speed to the asylum. These two gentlemen are expected!' The priests' fury when they arrived at the asylum was such that they were indeed taken for madmen and had a hard time extricating themselves. Don Bosco was left in peace after that.

The Pinardi Shed

Don Bosco was not mad, and since his vision was given by Our Lady herself it soon began to come true. The lease on the field where they currently met was coming to an end; if they could not find another venue then the group, which John now called the Oratory of Saint Francis de Sales, whom he had taken as his patron, would have to be disbanded. With a week to go, a man came to him with an offer of a shed for thirty lire a month in the Valdocco. When John went to inspect it he was dismayed. The shed hardly merited such a title. It was a broken-down, damp and muddy outhouse attached to a wretched one-storey hovel, the Pinardi house, with an iron balcony from which hung shreds of washing. It was on sloping ground so that one end of the shed was barely three feet above ground. Signor Pinardi was eager to rent it out and agreed to dig down into the ground to make more head space.

This is my house

However, it did have a major, though dubious, advantage. It was ideal for his ragamuffin tribe because no-one else would want it. The shed was in a damp and muddy field stretching from the side of the Refuge to a market at the other end, and with neighbours even more disreputable than they, there would be no complaints of noise and disruption. It was a dumping ground for broken fences and building debris, of rubbish heaps and garden refuse. The market, serving the poorest people of the city, was the haunt of thieves and pickpockets and even they did not go out at night without a weapon. The shed door looked straight into a disreputable tavern which was the secret meeting place of the militant anti-Catholic sect of the Waldensians.

Don Bosco signed the lease and on Easter Sunday 12th April 1846, as the bells rang out celebrating the Resurrection of Our Lord, John and his jubilant troop of boys poured into the field in the Valdocco. John nailed over the shed the title of what he would make of the poor hovel: *Haec est Domus Mea; Inde Gloria Mea* – This is My House; My Glory shall shine from it. He made it into a chapel with a wooden altar and a few benches, and it also doubled as a classroom and study room.

Collapse

Quietly Don Bosco started to add to these poor beginnings. He gradually rented more sheds and rooms nearby, which he turned into workrooms and classrooms.

He wanted to train as many boys as would benefit in trades that would provide them with a better prospect in life, such as tailoring, painting and carpentry. He began evening classes in Italian, French and Geography. He had been observing his boys and picked out the most intelligent and those who had already benefited most from his training to become teachers and assistants in their turn. This was a method he continued to use as his work expanded.

Then, with his dream starting to take shape, John collapsed with the stress of his heavy work load. Besides his work with the boys and orphans he heard endless confessions, he visited the sick and built up a wide circle of friends and benefactors who helped support his work. He did this in all weathers, in cold and heat, soaked in the rain, freezing in Winter, often missing his meals. In midsummer he collapsed and fainted with pneumonia, blood foaming from his lips. He was in rooms rented from the Marchesa; Don Calasso and Don Borel and his mother were warned that he might die and came immediately to his bedside. John's only prayer was for the will of God, but his boys all over Turin, now five hundred of them, were storming heaven, praying wherever they were - on their building sites and at their work benches, - saying the rosary, offering their Masses. John had no chance against the fervour of his boys, and he started to recover. The first time he left his room the boys carried him shoulder high, scattering flowers on the road. They proceeded, with singing and music, to the shed at Valdocco, where they sang a *Te Deum* that could be heard a quarter of a mile away.

Recovery

For a while John returned to the Becchi farm to recuperate, and an incident there illustrated how his reputation was spreading. Out walking one day a young man stepped out in front of him brandishing a knife and demanding his money or his life. John looked at him and smiling, said, 'I have neither, but do you really want to harm Don Bosco?' The knife dropped from the man's hand as he recognised John as the young priest who had visited him in the Turin prison. Since his release from prison he had found it difficult to find work and had reverted to his old ways. John invited him home, introducing him to his mother and brother as a friend, although Margaret suspected what sort of a friend he was. Next morning John sent him on his way with a letter of recommendation that soon secured him a job.

He was eager to return to his boys but the problem was where to live on his return. The Marchesa had let out his room but he managed to rent part of the adjoining Pinardi house which had four small rooms and a tiny loft. With him came his mother: by now Anthony had his own farm, Joseph was managing the family farm, and her mother-in-law had died, so she had no ties. Now her son John – and his horde of boys – needed her.

It was not an easy transition for her when she could have looked forward to a quiet retirement. The Pinardi house was in a terrible condition, so she set to and brought it up to her own standards of cleanliness. She brought her precious bridal dowry with her, and with great renunciation later cut up her wedding dress to make altar cloths and, when money was desperately needed, sold her jewellery.

She came as Don Bosco's housekeeper, but soon found herself in the role that was to be hers for the rest of her life – mother to all his boys, many of whom had never known a mother's care before. To all of them she became their Mamma Margaret.

Love for the strays

An incident not long after this opened up a new development in Don Bosco's vision for his boys. It was in the Spring of 1847 and he was returning home in the evening after collecting money for his Oratory. A gang of boys saw his clerical garb and began to call after him 'Caw, caw,' the anti-clerical crow insult often hurled after priests and religious. Don Bosco stopped and smiled at them, drawing nearer to them until the insults stopped. None would own up to who had been shouting after him.

'What's the trouble, friends?'

'If you are a friend, prove it,' retorted one of the boys.

'How can I do that, son?'

To general laughter one of them piped up,

'Buy us a drink!'

The Alps Tavern was nearby, so Don Bosco invited them along and stood them all a drink. Then he asked of them only one thing. He didn't mind insults being hurled at him, he said, but 'When some of you use language that blasphemes God, that does matter. It is foolish and ungrateful. You depend on Almighty God for all you have. The favour I ask is that you promise me not to use such language again.'

They promised. He then sent them off home to their beds – but most had no bed to go to. John then realised he had room to spare in his house and invited the twelve who had no lodgings to come with him. Margaret and he made up straw mattresses for them, only to discover in the morning that they had all left, taking the mattresses with them.

The first boarders

It was a few weeks later, in May, that his hospitality bore better fruit. It had been raining heavily that evening when there was a knock on the door and a boy of about fourteen, dripping wet, stood outside asking for something to eat. His story was a common one. His name was Michael Fassio, he was from Valsesia, some way from Turin, and he had come to the city looking for work as a bricklayer but had run out of money. Of course they invited him in and offered him a bed for the night, but John told him the story of how the gang of boys had let him down. Could they trust him?

'Father, I'm not a thief,' he replied. They took the risk, but Margaret took the precaution of locking the kitchen door and keeping the key in her pocket. John taught him his evening prayers which he had forgotten. He was still there when they all woke up and in a few days had found work but continued to stay with the Boscos. Michael Fassio was the first Salesian boarder.

Within a few days he was joined by others, and soon bought up the remainder of the Pinardi house. This, of course, meant that even more money was needed to provide for his charges, and John would tramp in all weathers from house to house collecting money for them, although some of the boys were apprentices or had jobs that enabled them to pay something towards their keep. Margaret would cook for them and everyone would sit around the courtyard eating whatever they had, the paucity of their meal made up for with song, laughter and comradeship.

Training his boys

Don Bosco was extending his operations. At the heart of what he gave the boys was the Christian faith, instruction in the Faith, Mass, the Rosary, devotions, prayer. Brief spiritual talks of five minutes, no more, would intersperse their work and play, so that none would become bored but everything would be infused with a Christian ethos and outlook. Confession and frequent Communion were encouraged. Don Bosco said that if children were given only an education and taught good manners they would produce only an affectionate, perfected, intelligent animal. They needed the deeper formation of character that the love of God would give them.

To him, music and the creative arts were a vital part of the boys' development, so they formed their own band and set up a little theatre where they put on plays. Children who could not read or write would be given lessons in the basics of education; others would be taught a practical skill that would enable them to obtain a good job. When they went out to work or took up an apprenticeship Don Bosco would inspect their place of work to make sure they were well treated and not exploited.

Boys should be loved

What principles lay behind Don Bosco's outstanding success with his boys? An incident years before deeply influenced him. It occurred when he had gone with his mother to Don Sismondo, his parish priest, to discuss making his First Communion. He was a somewhat aloof and withdrawn priest and John had been upset that Father Sismondo had ignored him and spoken curtly to them. In tears, John had asked his mother afterwards why the priest had ignored him.

'Priests are very busy people,' his mother replied. 'They have lots of problems to think about. You can't expect them to waste time on little boys like you.'

John was not to be persuaded. 'If I became a priest,' he responded, 'I shall never treat little boys like that.' This resolution would have been reinforced during his seminary days when the professors, in a somewhat Jansenistic atmosphere, kept themselves apart from the seminarians. Now a priest himself, Don Bosco was always and everywhere open and available to everyone and above all to his boys, whom he treated with the utmost respect, seeing their unique individuality and their potential. He said that the boys should be loved, and know that they were loved.

Asked one day if he had ever had recourse to physical punishment he held up his two hands and said, 'How could I strike a boy with these hands that have held the Body of the Lord?' The example of his old friend Comollo had been well learnt. He said that the severest punishment he had to mete out to a boy who proved intractable and a disruptive influence was to have to send him away from the Institute, and then, he said, it was like cutting off one of his own limbs. Nevertheless, he could be decisive when a boy needed to be expelled. Years later, when his Oratories had spread, the director of the Barcelona Oratory, by a feat of bilocation, received a visit from Don Bosco – who was in Turin at the time – and was told to send away three of his boys as soon as possible. Disturbed, because he had seen no evidence of wrongdoing, Fr Branda delayed the expulsion until he received another, internal, order from Don Bosco. He interviewed the boys, and realised they did indeed merit expulsion and they left that evening.

Love and trust

Between them, Margaret and John gave their boys the fatherly and motherly love that most of them had never had. The Oratory was a true family, where laughter, music, faith, work and self-respect were paramount. The boys trusted him.

One confession day Jemmy, a new arrival, wanted to make a General Confession; to make sure he didn't forget anything he wrote down all his sins in a book, but during the day he lost it. The boys brought him to Don Bosco, his face swollen with crying; the boys laughed as he confessed, 'I've lost my sins!' John, told him that he was a happy boy to go to heaven in that state. 'No, I've lost the book with all my sins in it!' Smiling, John produced the missing book from his cassock; Jemmy's sins were safe with him. Happy now, Jemmy retorted, 'If I'd known, this evening I would just have said I accuse myself of all the sins you have in your pocket!' This was the sort of relationship Don Bosco had with his boys.

His name was becoming so well known now that boys knew where to go if they were in danger. One day he was confronted by an angry father who demanded that Don Bosco should give his son back. John denied all knowledge of him, but one of the Oratory boys has seen him climb up into a tree to escape his father, who beat and ill-treated him. The father threatened to call the police and Don Bosco urged him to do so. 'And when the officer comes I shall lodge a complaint against you, charging you with ill-treating your son.' The father left, grumbling and cursing, and the boys now tried to coax the child down out of the tree, only to find that he had fainted with the terror of it all. Don Bosco climbed up a ladder to bring him down, but he screamed and kicked with fright as he came to.

'Don't be afraid, look at me,' soothed John. 'I'm Don Bosco. Your friend.' That was enough to calm the child, who became yet another boarder at the Oratory.

A prison outing

His work with boys was not confined to the Oratory. From the very beginning of his ministry Don Bosco had been deeply concerned about the condition of boys in the Turin prison. 'I was horrified to see so many healthy, strong and lively youths between twelve and eighteen years of age without occupation, crawling with lice, deprived of both spiritual and material nourishment,' he told Father Cafasso, and their welfare was a major part of his ministry.

In May 1855 he preached an eight-day retreat to them. Resistant at first, they soon fell under Don Bosco's spell and as the Retreat drew to a close hundreds of them lined up to make their Confession to him and receive Holy Communion. Don Bosco then went to the Warden with an outrageous request. 'Will you allow me to take the boys for an outing in the country?'

'Don Bosco, if I listened to your astonishing proposal, I might as well close down this Reformatory as there would be nobody left in it. I might as well go down to the Zoo and let out all the wild birds, telling them to be sure to return at five o'clock. Of course I can't approve your ridiculous suggestion.'

Don Bosco was not one to give in easily and eventually the Warden agreed to pass the request on to the Minister of State, Signor Rattazzi, who, to his amazement, gave his permission.

'These boys are where they ought to be, in a state of grace,' John reassured the sceptical Warden. I know how to treat them. I will put each one of them on his honour to return at the end of the day. They will be back, I promise you.'

The lads went wild with joy at the news of the picnic and outing, and they promised each other that anyone who fell out of line would be torn to pieces. The following morning a pack horse laden with food led a procession of three hundred young criminals through the streets of Turin, out into the countryside. In the evening, all three hundred returned.

Attacks and Persecution

Nineteenth-century Italy was in a social and religious
ferment, with growing anti-Catholic movements springing
up in opposition to the Church. In the Piedmont, Don
Bosco's home ground, one such was the Waldensians.
They had originated in the Middle Ages, a movement that
had once had papal approval as they strove to bring back a
life of poverty and simplicity to the Church, similar to the
Franciscans. The only stipulation the Pope made was that
they should be active in parishes only with the permission
of the Parish Priest. The Waldensians disobeyed this
simple injunction, and with this one act of disobedience
grew further and further away from the Church. They
suffered often severe persecution as a result, and in the
sixteenth century joined the Protestant movement.

In Don Bosco's time they became especially active,
vigorously distributing anti-Catholic tracts, pamphlets
and polemics against the Church. Don Bosco decided to
respond in kind and took up his pen to write in defence of
the Faith – he became a prolific writer, penning some 700
works of different kinds. For every tract produced by the
Waldensians John wrote one in defence.

One day he heard that one of his old boys who had
been drawn into the Waldensian faith was near to death

and he went to see him. The pastor tried to block Don Bosco from entering the room or of speaking to him, but John said that he wanted only to speak to him – it was up to the boy to choose whether to remain a Waldensian or return to the Catholic faith – the pastor could not deny freedom of conscience, so Don Bosco asked the boy what he would choose.

'Oh, it's you, Don Bosco! I was born Catholic, I want to die Catholic.' The pastor accepted defeat, put on his hat, left the room, and allowed the boy to be reconciled to the Church.

Grigio

The pastor accepted defeat but others did not. In the street Don Bosco was subjected to insults and verbal abuse. He was set upon and beaten up but managed, with his great strength, to fight off his assailants. Another time he was fired at and the bullet ripped through his cassock. When he was called out to visit a dying man and offered a glass of Asti, John at first thought to drink it, then reconsidered and offered it to a boy posted at the door, who refused to drink it. It was poisoned. Visiting another allegedly dying person, the woman turned out to be a decoy; he was set upon by a gang who rained down blows upon him. He shielded his head with a chair, hurled it at the men and managed to escape.

Sometimes ruffians were hired to attack him. One such came at him with a knife, and when he was arrested confessed he had been hired to feign madness and stab Don Bosco. When he was offered double the payment to defend him he accepted with alacrity and became John's bodyguard for a while.

Then an incident occurred that made a bodyguard unnecessary. One autumn evening in 1852 he was returning across a piece of deserted wasteland when he noticed that he was being followed by a large dog. Worried at first, he called to the dog which came up to him and proved to be friendly and accompanied him home. It then turned round and went away. It saved Don Bosco's life on at least three occasions. One dark and foggy winter's night he walked into an ambush. Some men rushed at him and threw a cloak over him, stuffing his mouth with a gag to prevent him from calling out. Then he heard an enormous growl and Grigio, the Grey One, as they called him now, launched himself at the gang until the terrified men made their escape.

It would accompany Don Bosco when he was called out at night and occasionally would come into the house, where the boys would play with him. But on those occasions he came only with a purpose, to prevent the priest from going out. One evening John had to give up trying to leave the house because Grigio growled every time he approached the door. Shortly afterwards a neighbour came to warn him that he had overheard plans to attack him.

Grigio was there as long as the persecution continued. He appeared ten years after that when Don Bosco was visiting the Moglia farm and wished for protection. His final appearance was thirty one years after his first appearance, (when John had lost his way and needed his protection again).

Satanic attacks

These attacks ceased eventually, but another form of attack began in February 1862. Colleagues noticed that he was looking tired and drawn, and Don Bosco admitted that he had not been able to sleep for four or five nights because of satanic disturbance. He would hear a loud voice in his ear, loud noises, gushing wind, books and paperwork scattered, furniture dancing about; his bed would be shaken violently, the bedclothes torn off. Whenever he tried to sleep he would be woken up. John was level-headed and not given lightly to suspect the work of the devil. When he was a young boy at home, the whole family was terrified for several days by the sound of claw-like steps, crashing sounds and dragging chains coming from the attic above their heads. Only John was brave enough to climb up the ladder to investigate, saying even at that young age that there must be some rational explanation. There was. A hen, pecking corn, had become trapped underneath a sieve and had spent several frantic days trying to escape.

Now he knew that he was the target of diabolic attack. At one point he went to stay with the Bishop of Ivrea hoping to escape from the disturbances, but after a few days they followed him there. On his return he told some of his closest assistants what was happening, and they begged him to perform an exorcism, but he refused. 'If I send him away from me, he will attack my boys,' he replied, because he realised that this was what had happened during the few days' respite at the bishop's house.

A year later, after the attacks had ceased, John told some of his older boys about it. 'I'm not afraid of the devil!' one of them boasted, adding that he would soon make short work of him.

'Silence!' ordered Don Bosco loudly and authoritatively. To him it was no light matter. Some suggested he make the sign of the Cross, use holy water, but although these helped they would avail only for a moment, John explained, but added that he had found the way to make him run away and not appear for a good long while. He refused to say what that means was, but it could have been what Our Lord said, Prayer and fasting, and also penance, something he did not want his boys to undertake lest they lack the necessary discretion.

Expansion

It was little wonder that the devil took such a malign interest in the work of Don Bosco, because it was expanding rapidly. More Oratories were opened in rapid succession and then Urban Rattazzi, a Minister of State, suggested that he put his work on a more permanent basis and form a Society. This intervention was all the more remarkable in that Rattazzi was rabidly anti-clerical and had been instrumental in suppressing religious orders and driving them from the kingdom. However, he was fair-minded enough to see the value of Don Bosco's work, and despite the Law of Suppression, guaranteed that the Government would not oppose the setting up of the Society.

As soon as news of this proposal was made known, John had no lack of willing volunteers. He also had enthusiastic approval from his bishop, who was in exile in France, and who further suggested that he should also seek papal approbation. Consequently, in February 1858 Don Bosco set off for Rome with his secretary, Michael Rua, although it was 8th March before he obtained an audience with the Pope, Pius IX. The Pope also gave him his approval and blessing, sending him back to Turin with twenty five gold coins with which to treat his boys.

Despite the Pope's approval the Vatican wheels ground very slowly and Don Bosco came up against determined opposition. Many thought it was demeaning for priests to join in play with their charges. Others considered there were too many religious congregations already. Some frowned on John's educational methods that put so much emphasis in giving so much freedom for his boys to develop.

When, after two years of waiting, no official approbation had been received, John decided to start things off himself and began to organise his Congregation, with himself elected as Superior General. Two years later twenty two young men took temporary vows for three years. By the time official approbation was given in 1874 the Salesian Society was fully formed. Besides the novices, the seminarians, the priests and brothers who formed the core of the Society, other branches were also in place.

Salesian Co-Operators

Very early on, Mother Margaret had obviously found it impossible to cope single-handedly with her burgeoning crowd of boys, and around her had gathered men and women who took on the tasks of cooking, cleaning, maintaining the grounds, fundraising, and collaborating in the work of the Salesians. Gradually, these associates took on a lay ministry of their own, a kind of Third Order, and in 1876 were officially established as the Union of Salesian Co-Operators. Don Bosco also set up an Institute of Late Vocations among these collaborators, a real innovation at the time.

Basilica of Our Lady, Help of Christians

As the approbation dragged on Don Bosco turned his attention to yet another dream of his. He would build a great Basilica dedicated to Our Lady, Help of Christians. This title had long been John's favoured term for Our Lady. If funds were hard to come by to pay for his many projects, it was Our Lady, Help of Christians, who would provide. If his work seemed hard and unrewarding, he had no doubts, because everything was in her hands. If someone was cured of an illness, then it was Our Lady, Help of Christians who had done it. Moreover, he was buoyed up by a dream he had had some years before. 'You need a field?' Our Lady said to him. 'Here is the field. A chapel? Here it is. A house for your children? Again, here it is. Refectories, dormitories, workshops, classes, arcades? I give them to you. A great church dedicated to me? It is before you, and on the very spot where Saints Solutor, Adventor and Octavius, martyrs of the Theban Legion, were struck down.'

All but the church he already had, so he knew he would have that too, but as always he would co-operate with Our Lady in working for it. He was tireless in begging for money from princes and businessmen, from clergy and laity, travelling all over the country gathering funds. The background of this was rising anti-clericalism, but Don Bosco had a weapon in his armoury that atheism could never have.

A certain Commander Cotta was dying but John reassured him he would not die. 'My church needs you. How much will you give Our Lady for her church?' The Commander pledged two thousand lire for six months, the sum was agreed and he recovered. A man with severe rheumatism asked for a cure. He said he was unable to get to the bank because of his condition, but John persuaded him to try; he rode in his carriage to the bank and returned with the money and cured.

His boys, too, prayed hard for the church, and Don Bosco made sure that it was a little boy's hand, Emmanuel Fassati, who laid the final stone at the top of the dome. It was finally consecrated on 19th June, 1868. Over half the money had been given in thanksgiving for favours, miracles and cures received through Our Lady, Help of Christians.

Daughters of Mary, Help of Christians

Don Bosco had always seen his work as being with boys, so when it was put to him that there were girls who needed his help just as much, he was very reluctant at first to consider the idea. He gradually came to realise, though, that they did indeed need his help, if not more so. He had an immense regard for chastity and purity, not only in his own life, but in his desire to encourage it in others, and girls could sometimes be at greater risk of losing their innocence.

Again, a dream he had pointed the way ahead. In the dream a crowd of small girls ran and shouted and jumped around him, asking him to take care of them. 'I cannot do anything for you,' he replied, 'Trust in God's providence.'

'Must we roam the streets, then, at the mercy of every temptation?'

Then Our Lady stood before him, saying to him, 'These also are my children. I give them to you.' What Our Lady gave to him he could not refuse.

On a bright October day in 1856 Don Bosco, mounted on a white horse with a caravan of boys heralded by drums, came to meet with the parish priest of Mornese, Don Pestarino, and talk about an Association he had set up under the patronage of Mary Immaculate. Girls, most of whom were orphans, would be taught to read and write, to sew and to pray. At first, Don Bosco felt it was not for him, but again he gradually came to understand that it was indeed his concern.

One of their number, Maria Dominica Mazzarello, gradually formed a small community from the girls to further this work. Don Bosco was there on 5th August, 1872, when the community made their first vows and others were received as novices in the Congregation of Daughters of Mary Help of Christians, affiliated with the Salesian Order.

The Miracle Worker of Turin

Through Don Bosco's own holiness, miracles flowed. He visited the Mother Superior of the Convent of the Blessed Sacrament, who had been bed-ridden for four years. Don Bosco assured her she would be cured by that evening, and his only request was that she should visit him that evening to thank God. A carriage duly drew up at the Oratory that evening bearing a grateful nun.

A young girl who had been blind for two years came with her mother to pray at the Church of Our Lady, Help of Christians, and then sought out Don Bosco. He took out of his pocket a medal of Our Lady, and asked the girl to describe it, which she did, her sight restored.

A mother brought her seven year old boy to John for his blessing, and explained that the child had been crippled from birth. John blessed him, then walked to the other end of the room and invited him to come to him without his crutches. Encouraged by his mother, the boy took a couple of hesitant steps that brought him, cured, into Don Bosco's arms.

John encouraged everyone to have confidence in Our Lady, Help of Christians. In 1869 seven of his boys fell ill with smallpox. He came into the infirmary and asked them if they had confidence in Our Lady.

'Yes, Father,'

'Then get up and join your companions having a good time downstairs.'

Six of them got up, dressed, and joined the rest of the boys downstairs, cured, where prizes were being distributed. The first prize went to the seventh boy who did not have enough confidence to believe Don Bosco, and the illness had to take its usual course.

One of the most amazing miracles occurred to a young boy called Charles, who was already dead. He had wanted to make his final confession to Don Bosco, who was away at the time, and returned only twelve hours after Charles had died. He entered the room where the boy's body had already been laid out, the face covered with a veil. John knelt by his bed and called his name loudly, and the boy's head moved, although his body remained stiff and cold in death. Wrapped in his burial cloths Charles made his confession to Don Bosco, only his head moving. The priest asked him if he wanted to return to them or go to God, and Charles exclaimed emphatically that he wanted to be with God. Then the coldness of death spread once again to his face.

A feast of chestnuts

Other miracles were more homely, especially where his boys were concerned. Don Bosco had promised them a feast of chestnuts on All Souls Day, after they had processed to the cemetery to pray for the dead. He had given three bags to the cook, but on their return found the cook had cooked only one bag, not nearly enough to feed four hundred boys. Never mind; John prayed and began doling out the chestnuts, a full cap for each boy; finally, there was just one portion left, for Don Bosco. A feast of chestnuts on All Souls Day became an abiding celebration in all the Salesian houses.

Another day, a Feast Day when all the boys would receive Communion, the sacristan remembered, to his horror, that he had not put out another ciborium for consecration. There would not be enough Hosts for them all. Don Bosco noticed, too, prayed quietly and distributed Communion to all the boys out of the one, half filled ciborium.

Sadly, in the autumn of 1856 his mother Margaret fell ill with pneumonia. John heard her confession and gave her the Last Sacraments, and his brother Joseph was summoned from Castelnuovo. Her boys gathered round her bed, she told Joseph to raise his sons as farmers unless they had a vocation to the priesthood; to John she gave much advice on how the Oratory should develop. 'Seek the glory of God, not elegance or splendour, but have poverty as your base. Many love poverty for others, but not for themselves,' she observed shrewdly. 'Show by example not just by commands to others.' In the early hours of the morning on 25th November, she slipped quietly away to the Lord she loved, and John, despite his intense grief, knew that he now had another powerful advocate in heaven. In the morning he broke the news to his weeping boys; 'We have lost our mother, but I am sure she will help us from her place in Paradise. She was a saint.'

In 1860, his great friend and Confessor, Don Cafasso died, and in 1876 another of his great priest friends, Don Borel, was killed in an accident. All these bereavements were a great sorrow to him, but he was seeing a new generation grow up and growing in holiness. Surely the greatest miracles flowing through Don Bosco were those of conversion and holiness. One of the first fruits was Dominic Savio.

Dominic Savio

Every year in October John would take a group of his boys on a camping holiday to Becchi, putting them up in his brother Joseph's hayloft. In 1854 a boy of twelve came along with his father from the neighbouring village of Mondonio to speak with the priest. Such was the reputation of the Oratories and of Don Bosco that parents were now sending their own boys to them for the excellent training they received. The fees they paid helped, too, with the expenses of those who could not pay – no-one was turned away.

The young boy was Dominic Savio and he was already of exceptional holiness. When he made his First

Communion he made four resolutions, to go to Confession often and to Holy Communion when his confessor allowed; to make holy Sundays and Feast days special days; his friends would be Jesus and Mary; death rather than sin. Now, Dominic asked if he could return with Don Bosco to Turin to study.

'Well, there seems to be good stuff in you,' John replied.

'Good stuff for what?'

'To make a beautiful garment for Our Lord.' And he did. 'I recognised in that boy,' Don Bosco wrote later, 'a soul completely given to the Holy Spirit and I was deeply moved to see how much divine grace had already wrought in one so young.'

One day Dominic came into Don Bosco's room and insisted they that go out together. Walking along a street Dominic stopped at a particular door and told the priest to enter, saying 'This is where you are wanted.' Inside, the wife told him that her dying husband had lapsed from the Faith and wanted to die Catholic. Dominic would not say how he knew about this.

Dominic also told Don Bosco that he longed to go to Rome, as he had something he needed to tell the Pope. He was unable to do so, but when John went to see the Pope in 1858, the year after Dominic's death, he told the Pope of a vision Dominic had had. After Communion one day Dominic saw a country covered in thick mist, with people wandering around as if lost. He was told, 'This is

England.' Then he saw the Pope, Pius IX, carrying a torch that dispersed the mist and allowed the people to walk in daylight. 'This torch,' Dominic was then told, 'is the Catholic religion which is to illuminate England.' Shortly afterwards the Pope re-established the Catholic Hierarchy in England.

Dominic, now Saint Dominic Savio, died at the age of fifteen.

Michael Magone

Don Bosco was waiting for the train at Carmagnole one autumn evening. A noisy crowd of boys was deafening the people waiting for the train when from out of the tumult he heard a commanding voice of one of the boys that completely put a stop to the chaos. Intrigued, John went up to the crowd of boys who immediately scattered into the darkness, leaving only their ringleader, who stood belligerently facing down the priest, hands on his hips, demanding to know who had interrupted their play.

'A friend,' Don Bosco replied, 'who wants to join in with you. And who are you?'

'I,' said the thirteen year old lad solemnly, 'am Michael Magone, General of Recreation.'

He had made his Confession and First Communion, he said under John's questioning, although it was rather a joke to him; his occupation was idling, his father was dead and his mother earned what little she could to support the family. Yes, he said, he would like to learn a trade, and as Don Bosco's train was pulling into the station John gave Michael a medal and told him to speak to his parish priest who knew him and would direct him to the Oratory.

Don Bosco's little General came to the Oratory, but at first found it difficult to adjust. Finding him sad and withdrawn, John drew him gently aside.

'My dear Magon,' he said, 'will you tell me what's troubling you and let me share your sadness.' Michael continued to cry. 'Is this General Magone, chief of the band of Carmagnole! What a general, who can't find the words to tell me what the trouble is.' It transpired that Michael's conscience was troubling him about his past life, and with a general confession he became a new person. He was often to be found praying before the Blessed Sacrament that he would not slip back into his old ways. He did not; he died at the age of fifteen, taking with him a message to Our Lady that she would bless Don Bosco's work and ensure that none of those entrusted to his care would be lost.

Philip Rinaldo

Not all of Don Bosco's protegés died young! John had spotted the young Philip Rinaldo at the Mirabello Oratory.

'What if the Lord wants you to be a priest?' he asked the young boy. 'Think it over.' Philip thought it over and was adamant that he did not want to be a priest, ever, but

John was persistent over the years. Philip insisted that his poor health prevented him, as he had poor eyesight which triggered severe headaches.

'I promise you the headaches will cease, and you will have good enough eyesight to carry you through to the priesthood and through life.'

Now a young man, Don Bosco invited him to the Founder's day at the Borgo San Martino Salesian School and after the ceremony talked with him in the dining room. Philip testified that after they had spoken, John sat silently in prayer and his face gradually became radiant and far brighter than the sunlight streaming through the window. The effect faded after a few minutes, John excused himself and left the room. Philip soon afterwards entered the seminary. He went as a missionary to Australia and then Spain, and eventually was elected Superior General of the Order. Don Bosco knew his boys and of what they were capable.

Michael Rua

Don Bosco met Michael Rua when he was going to the Friar's School in Turin. The boys would always rush up to the priest for what he had in his pockets – sweets, nuts, toys, medals, holy pictures. To Michael he gave nothing; he only opened his empty hand, making a sign across it as if cutting it in half, saying 'This is for you, my little Michael.' Michael soon joined the oratory and was one of a group of boys whom John groomed as future priests. He became his first novice at the age of sixteen, and as we have seen accompanied Don Bosco to Rome to seek approbation for his Society. The 'half' Don Bosco promised him was to be John's right hand man, Vicar General of the Salesians and, finally, General of the Order.

Michael gave an impression of severity, and Don Bosco often told him to make himself loved. One day, Michael came up to a group gathered round Don Bosco who was telling them that he had had a dream. 'I dreamt I was in the sacristy and wanted to go to confession,' he said. 'I saw Fr Rua nearby, saying his breviary, but he looked so stern that my courage failed me. I was afraid he might be just as strict with me.'

Everyone laughed, but Fr Rua took it to heart. He worked so hard to achieve the fatherliness he so admired in Don Bosco, that he became a faithful replica of the saint. John, in his turn, admired the deep spirituality, the boundless energy and loyalty of his faithful lieutenant.

Worldwide

Don Bosco had another dream. In it he saw a city square with an enormous wheel in the centre. An angel set it spinning, one spin for every ten years of John's life. He alone could hear the noise of the first spin of the wheel; the next turn and all Piedmont heard it, then all Italy, then all Europe and finally the whole world. By 1861, the year of this dream, Oratories were spreading throughout a newly unified Italy, but Don Bosco was a man of great designs. On the wall of his room he had a big map of the world, over which he often pored. He was drawn most to South America, and he often spoke to his young followers of the foreign missions, inspiring them with his own enthusiasm.

In 1872 he had another dream in which he saw an immense, untilled field, over which a vast throng of tall, savage men were moving, almost naked, with dark, coppery skin, wearing long coats of fur. They carried lassos and long spears and were hunting, lumps of bleeding flesh on their spears. Then, in the distance, a long line of missionaries appeared; the savages immediately fell upon them and massacred them, but more appeared, then more, until the savages threw away their spears, sat down before the missionaries and were instructed in the Faith.

It was time to act, and Don Bosco received another sign. In 1854 one of his most promising boys, fifteen-year-old John Cagliero, had been dying of typhoid fever. John had come into Don Bosco's care three years earlier, after his father had died and his mother could no longer cope with a boy who was out of control. John's fierce loyalty to Don Bosco wrought the transformation. Now, the priest had another dream where he saw John lying on his deathbed tended lovingly by two of the savage men he had seen in his dream. A dove flew by and dropped and olive branch on the boy's pillow. Don Bosco therefore assured John that he would recover and become a missionary. In 1875, John Cagliero, now a priest, headed the first Salesian mission to Argentina. He died a Cardinal.

In France

That same year, 1875, Don Bosco travelled to France, and the Salesians expanded into France and then Spain; eventually they would be spread throughout the world.

His voyage through France was a triumph; everywhere throngs wild with excitement greeted his presence and listened to his sermons. He celebrated Masses, heard confessions, made converts, worked miracles. He did not mind the numberless photographs that were taken of him; without pride for himself, if they helped spread the glory of God then he was content.

In Paris a white-haired, elderly gentleman came to his room and straightforwardly declared that he refused to believe in the miracles that everyone was saying Don Bosco was working.

'Sir,' John replied, 'what do you believe about a future life?'

'We don't need to waste time discussing that! I'll talk about it when it comes.'

'Very soon the present will no longer be yours. You are bound to think of the eternal future, my friend. You have but a short span of life, but time enough to return to the Church.'

The elderly gentleman was silent for a while and said that he would think over what Don Bosco had said. He returned three days later and said that he did believe in eternal life and the immortality of the soul and hoped to die in the arms of a Catholic priest.

His visitor was Victor Hugo, who lived a year longer and asked for a priest on his deathbed, a dying request that was denied him by the atheist friends who surrounded him.

Humility and holiness

However great his fame, it never touched his profound humility. One day Don Bosco had occasion to severely reprimand Brother Joseph for laying soiled tablecloths when they were entertaining important visitors. The brother was so upset that he sent a note to John. 'I did not think it possible that you could become so angry with anyone, least of all with me,' he wrote and Don Bosco came to apologise to him. He reminded him of an incident that had happened a few days before. John had been late for supper after many hours in the confessional and all that was left for him was a plate of cold rice. The cook was just about to leave and responded, in the priest's hearing, to Brother Joseph's protest that Don Bosco needed something better, 'Don Bosco is no better than anyone else.' Brother Joseph apologised for the cook's remark, but John quietly started eating the cold mush. 'He's quite right,' he replied. 'I have no business being late.'

'What the cook said about me the other night was quite true,' he said now. 'I am no better than anyone else. I must try very much harder, and I want you to help me with your prayers.'

The Fire Dying Within

One day, a friend asked him how he could cope with his prodigious work load and the fundraising for all his various projects.

'I'm always going like a steam engine' he replied, then explained what he meant. 'It must have plenty of fire inside and something to feed the fire.' The fire was the fire of faith and confidence in God, he said, and without it empires fall and kingdoms shatter, and the work of man is useless.

A description of a normal day shows the enormous workload he assumed, and also the source of his inner fire – the Mass and prayer. After only five hours' sleep, he would rise in the early hours of the morning and pray for an hour. Before Mass, he reflected on the needs of his boys, of his work and the Church, and then hear the confessions of sometimes forty boys. After Mass he would go out into the courtyard to play uproarious games with his boys, have a word or a joke with them, looking for those who needed encouragement. After breakfast he spent the morning dealing with business. After lunch, he would spend an hour in prayer before working through his voluminous correspondence, and then would then set out into the city visiting the sick, soliciting money for his various projects, meeting with architects or bishops or governors. At meal times he was always at the disposal of his community and his boys who needed his advice or attention. After evening prayer and hymns, he was once again at their disposal. Even after midnight he might still have some writing to do. This was his life for forty five years until his body could no longer carry on.

The dying fire

The fire was gradually burning through even his indefatigable frame. In December 1884 Don Bosco became seriously ill but recovered. By this time there were more than eighty Oratories, the South American, French and Spanish missions were spreading, and the Pope asked him to build a basilica to the Sacred Heart in Rome, with all the fundraising effort this entailed.

In 1885 Don Bosco was seventy years old, and a doctor, Dr Fissore of Turin, examining him, said his heart was that of a 150 year old. Another doctor, Dr Combal, remarked that 'It is said, and I quite believe it, that Don Bosco worked miracles through the power of God, but the greatest miracle in my opinion is that he lives in this shattered state of health. He is like a garment worn out by use, which, if we wish to preserve, we must keep shut up in a wardrobe.'

In October 1887 he went to the Seminary of Foglizzo to give the habit to more than a hundred young Salesians, and whispered to Father Rua that next year he would have to perform the ceremony.

By the end of the year he was virtually confined to his room, unable to walk unaided, almost blind, his body shattered, watched over lovingly by his faithful Don Rua, and his other assistant, Father Durando. His room was a poorly furnished attic at the top of several flights of stairs with a room where his many visitors waited to see him. An altar was set up in the next room where he said Mass. On 24th December 1888 he received Viaticum, but lingered on, almost paralysed, into the New Year and the feast day of his patron, Saint Francis de Sales, 29th January. Work at the Oratory came to a halt while priests, brother, sisters and eight hundred of his boys filed past for one last glimpse of him. Throughout the city, on building sites, classrooms and work shops, prayers were said silently and together for their friend who had transformed so many lives. In the early hours of 31st January, bells tolled out from the Basilica of Our Lady, Help of Christians, to tell all that this great soul had slipped peacefully away.

The Great Ship

Dreams guided Don Bosco throughout his life, but one dream he had seems to point to beyond his own life.

In this prophetic dream he saw a vast expanse of sea in which were planted two enormous pillars a short distance apart from each other. On one pillar was an enormous Host, with a placard beneath *Salus Credentium* – Salvation of believers; on the other, slightly smaller pillar, was a statue of Our Lady with the inscription *Aulilium Christianorum* – Help of Christians.

On the sea was a multitude of battling ships fitted with beaks of iron, armed with cannons, firearms, incendiary devices and even books, all of them intent on just one target, a large, stately ship, shielded by an escort fleet, that they were ramming, firing at, hurling missiles, trying in every way to destroy. The Pope was the commanding general of the ship, who despite the attacks was intent on steering the ship into the safe harbour of the two pillars. At one point the Pope was hit and wounded, but another took his place. At last the ship reached the two pillars of the Eucharist and Our Lady, and was anchored firmly to them. Of the other ships on the sea some fled and collided with each other and were sunk. Others immediately tied up beside the great ship, while others waited awhile before doing so. Then perfect calm descended on the sea.

The Eucharist and Our Lady were the twin anchors of Don Bosco's life, and in this dream he was being shown that they are the twin anchors that will also hold the whole Church steady.

Francis de Sales

Francis' vocation and intrepid missionary work in France and Geneva were born and tested in the turmoil of European religious wars and the Reformation. Despite poor health, his fine mind, legal training and powerful pen, coupled with his great faith and zeal made him a persuasive and effective debater against the Calvinism of his time.

A contemporary of Jane Frances de Chantal and Vincent de Paul, Francis (1567-1622) became Bishop of Geneva, where he died, exhausted, at only 55. This booklet introduces the reader to his writings, samples of which are included.

Barry Midgley, a retired Headmaster, has spent most of his professional life in Catholic education. He has published several titles with CTS and lives in East Anglia.

ISBN: 978 1 86082 521 7

CTS Code: B708

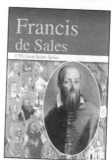